Credit C... MATH

REM 5241

AUTHOR: Sue LaRoy

A TEACHING RESOURCE FROM

©2019, 2018
Copyright by Remedia Publications, Inc.
All Rights Reserved. Printed in the U.S.A.

The purchase of this product entitles the individual teacher to reproduce copies for classroom use.
The reproduction of any part for an entire school or school system is strictly prohibited.

www.rempub.com

REMEDIA PUBLICATIONS, INC.
SCOTTSDALE, AZ

This product utilizes innovative strategies and proven methods to improve student learning. The product is based upon reliable research and effective practices that have been replicated in classrooms across the United States. Information regarding the Common Core State Standards this product meets is available at www.rempub.com/standards.

INTRODUCTION

Credit Card Math provides students with an opportunity to improve real-life math skills as they learn about credit cards and how they are used.

The first section of this book presents comprehensive, practical information about credit cards: what they are, how to apply for a credit card, what a credit score is, how to interpret a statement, what it means to use a credit card responsibly, and much more. Follow-up activities will test student understanding of important information.

The math section of this book features many practical everyday-life situations involving the use of a credit card to pay for goods and services. Students will read word problems and decide whether to add, subtract, multiply, and/or divide to arrive at a solution. The book progresses in difficulty. Several pages require students to know how to figure percentages, round to the nearest hundredths place, and fill in graphs and a pie chart. Activities also include shopping online using a credit card.

The vocabulary section consists of a glossary of terms relating to credit cards. Activities following the glossary serve to test student understanding of the words and phrases. The vocabulary follow-up activities as well as the review on page 18 may be used as a pre- or post-test.

TABLE OF CONTENT

SECTION ONE: Comprehensive, Practical Credit Card Information 1-17
Types of Credit Cards, Application Forms, Account Statements, Credit Scores

SECTION TWO: MATH ACTIVITIES 19-53
    Fact Sheet #1 Activities 19-25
    filling out forms, add/subtract money, graphs

    Fact Sheet #2 Activities 26-33
    filling out forms, add/subtract, multiply/divide money, graphs

    Fact Sheet #3 Activities 34-41
    filling out forms, add/subtract, multiply/divide money, percentages, rounding

    Fact Sheet #4 Activities 42-50
    filling out forms, add/subtract, multiply/divide money, percentages, fractions, rounding, pie chart

    Use Your Own Credit Card Activities 51-53

SECTION THREE: VOCABULARY ACTIVITIES 54-59
    Glossary 54-55
    Vocabulary Activities 56-59

ANSWER KEY 60-62

WHAT IS A CREDIT CARD?

A credit card is a small card with a **magnetic stripe** on the back. It is given out by a bank or business. Most credit cards have a small **microchip** on the front. This is for extra security and to prevent **fraud**.

A credit card allows you to borrow money from a bank to make purchases. You can pay for most anything using a credit card including food, clothing, medicine, household goods, and much more.

You must be approved for a credit card. When you receive your card, you will see your name and a number on the front. No two people have the same number. This number is your **account number**. With this number, the bank will keep track of the money you borrow.

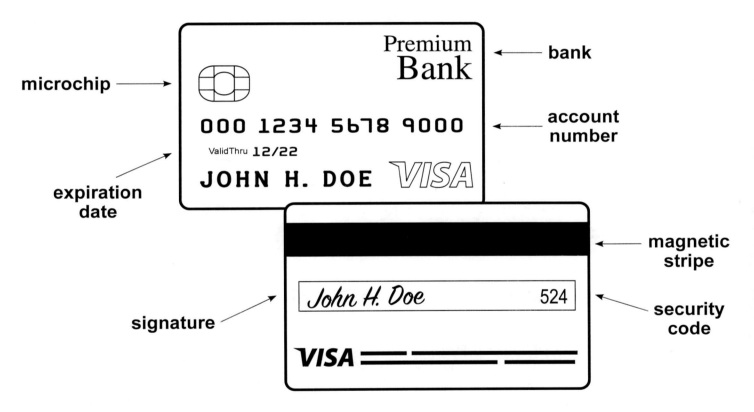

Also on the front is an **expiration date**. After that date, you can no longer use the card. If you have been making payments on time and have not gone over your credit limit, you will receive a new card. Your **credit limit** is the maximum amount the bank will let you borrow.

You must sign your name on the back of the card. Next to your signature is a 3-digit CVV number. CVV stands for Card Verification Value. This number is a **security code**. The security code helps to prevent fraud. When you purchase something online or by phone, you will be asked for this code.

MORE ABOUT CREDIT CARDS

Buying on credit means that you are borrowing money from the place that gave you the credit card. You must pay back all the money you borrowed.

If you pay back all the money within 25 to 30 days, you will not have to pay extra. If you don't pay it back in that time period, you must pay interest. **Interest** is a percentage of the money you owe the bank—on top of what you borrowed.

Types of Credit Cards

Visa® and **MasterCard**® are the two main types of credit cards. Visa® and MasterCard® do not give out credit cards. They are big technology companies that provide a payment network to banks for purchases made with credit cards. They do this in a fast, reliable, and secure way. Visa® and MasterCard® credit cards can be used in thousands of businesses in more than 200 countries around the world.

Business Credit Cards

A credit card given out by a business is a little different. While you will still have a credit limit on the card, you can only charge purchases at that business. For example, a Target credit card can only be used to buy things from Target.

Name _____

Use information from pages 1 and 2 to answer the questions.

1. Why do most companies put a small microchip on the front of their credit cards?
   _____
   _____

2. What is the security code on the sample bank credit card?
   _____
   _____

3. Name three things that you can buy using a credit card.
   _____
   _____

4. What is the account number on the sample bank credit card?
   _____
   _____

5. What happens if you do not pay back all of the money that you borrowed within 25 to 30 days?
   _____
   _____

6. Name the two main types of credit cards that banks give out.
   _____
   _____

7. How are credit cards given out by businesses different than credit cards given out by banks?
   _____
   _____

8. How do you know how long you can use your credit card?
   _____
   _____

HOW TO GET A CREDIT CARD

To get a credit card from a bank or a business, you must first fill out an application form. The form will ask for your name, address, and social security number. As well, you will be asked about your job and income. You may also have to provide **credit references**.

The bank or business giving out the card must approve you. Approval depends mostly on your **credit score**. Your salary, how long you have been on the job, and your credit references are also very important. If you are approved, you will receive your card in the mail.

If you do not have a **credit history**, you may still be able to get one of the following types of credit cards.

Student Card

Some companies have special student credit cards. To apply you must be at least 18 years old. You must have your own income. Your credit limit will depend on how much you make. You will be responsible for paying the **debt**.

Authorized User Card

An authorized user card is a card with your name on it but it is part of someone else's credit card account. You can use it to make purchases. The primary cardholder is the person responsible for paying the debt.

Secured Card

To get a secured card you must give the company a cash deposit. This deposit is usually the same amount as your credit limit. You can use this card like any other credit card. You are responsible for the debt. The cash deposit protects the company if you do not pay off the debt.

CREDIT LIMITS

When a credit card is given out, a credit limit is set. A **credit limit** is how much money you can borrow using that card. A credit limit can be anywhere from $500 to $10,000 or more. Your credit limit depends on the type of bank or business that is giving out the card, your credit score, how much money you make, and how much debt you have.

Credit Card Math

Name _____

Use information from page 4 to answer the questions.

1. What is the first thing you have to do to get a credit card?
   _____
   _____

2. Name two things that will help you get approved for a credit card.
   _____
   _____

3. How old do you have to be to get a student credit card?
   _____
   _____

4. How do you get your credit card once you have been approved?
   _____
   _____

5. Who is responsible for paying the debt on an authorized user card?
   _____
   _____

6. How is a secured credit card different from other types of cards?
   _____
   _____

7. What is a credit limit?
   _____
   _____

8. Name two things that affect your credit limit.
   _____
   _____

GOLD STANDARD BANK

CREDIT CARD APPLICATION

APPLICANT INFORMATION				
LAST NAME: Fernandez		FIRST NAME: Alice	MI: M	BIRTH DATE: 06/12/2001
SOCIAL SECURITY NO.: 001-23-4512				TELEPHONE: 480-555-8181
CURRENT ADDRESS: 5815 S. Sterling St.			APT. NO.: 336A	HOW LONG? ___ Yrs. 3 Months
CITY / STATE / ZIP: Tempe, AZ 85287				☐ Rent ☐ Own ☐ Live with Others
PREVIOUS ADDRESS: 10811 East Portabello Ave.			APT. NO.	HOW LONG? 16 Yrs. 5 Months
CITY / STATE / ZIP: Mesa, AZ 85260				☐ Rent ☐ Own ☐ Live with Others

EMPLOYMENT INFORMATION			
CURRENT EMPLOYER: Starbucks		POSITION: Barista	2 Yrs. 1 Months
STREET ADDRESS: 420 S. Mill Street			PHONE NUMBER: 480-966-7228
CITY / STATE / ZIP: Tempe, AZ 85287			GROSS MONTHLY INCOME: $1,500
OTHER INCOME SOURCE: Dog Walker			MONTHLY AMOUNT: $200

CREDIT REFERENCES	
CHECKING ACCOUNT	SAVINGS ACCOUNT
BANK: Gold Standard Bank	BANK: Premium Bank
ACCOUNT NO.: 10005585	ACCOUNT NO.: 50001158
LANDLORD'S NAME (if renting): Raphael Arafa	MONTHLY RENT: $750

NAMES OF CREDITORS (List banks, department stores, finance companies, amount owed, and monthly payment amount.)

Not Applicable.

Name _____

Use information from page 6 to answer the questions.

1. Alice Fernandez filled out the sample credit application. What is her social security number?
    _____

2. How long has Alice lived at her current address?
    _____

3. What year was Alice born?
    _____

4. What was Alice's previous address?
    _____
    _____

5. Who is Alice's current employer and how long has she worked there?
    _____

6. What company is Alice trying to get credit from?
    _____

7. How much does Alice make each month from her other income source?
    _____

8. How much is Alice's monthly rent?
    _____

9. Where does Alice have her checking account?
    _____

HOW TO USE A CREDIT CARD

Once you have your credit card, you can use it three main ways.

IN PERSON
When you purchase something at a store the cashier will swipe your card or you will insert the microchip into a **credit card machine** at the register.

BY PHONE
You can purchase things or pay bills over the phone. Just give your name, account number, expiration date, and **security code**.

ONLINE
You can also purchase items online. When it comes time to pay for your purchase, fill out the credit card information at checkout.

NEW CREDIT CARD TECHNOLOGY

RADIO FREQUENCY IDENTIFICATION (RFID)
RFID is a small chip found on some credit cards. It allows you to tap the card to the credit card machine to pay.

NEAR-FIELD COMMUNICATION (NFC)
NFC technology is similar to RFID. Except you don't need your credit card in-hand to pay. Instead, tap your smart watch, phone, or device to the credit card machine to pay.

Credit Card Math

CREDIT CARD ACCOUNT STATEMENT

Once you start using your credit card, you will receive an account statement each month. You will receive this statement either in the mail or online. This statement will show how much you owe and what your **minimum payment** is for the month. It is important to read this statement carefully and make sure your payment is made by the **due date** shown.

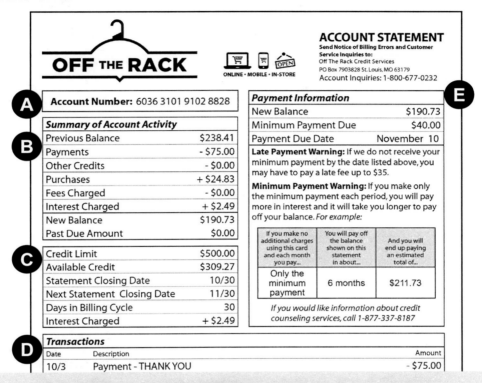

YOUR STATEMENT WILL INCLUDE

A. your account number
B. previous balance and any payments that have been made
C. your credit limit, your current balance, and your available credit
D. a list of **transactions** that include current purchases both online and in-store
E. your minimum payment and the date it is due

RESPONSIBLE CREDIT CARD USE

To use your card responsibly, avoid overspending. Make smaller purchases that you can afford. Try to pay off your **balance** each month. Do not go over your credit limit. Make sure you make your payment on or before the due date. You can sign up for email or text payment reminders. You can also set up automatic bill payment from your checking account. All of these things will help you establish a good **credit score**.

Name _____

Use information from pages 8 and 9 to answer the questions.

1. How do you purchase something online using your credit card?
   _____
   _____

2. What information do you have to give to purchase something over the phone using your credit card?
   _____
   _____

3. What is the main purpose of a credit card statement?
   _____
   _____

4. How do you use a credit card with an RFID chip?
   _____
   _____

5. How do you know when to make your credit card payment?
   _____
   _____

6. What is a good way to avoid overspending on your credit card?
   _____
   _____

7. What are two things you can do to remember when your payment is due?
   _____
   _____

8. Why is it important to pay make your payment on time each month?
   _____
   _____

Credit Card Math

ONLINE • MOBILE • IN-STORE

ACCOUNT STATEMENT

Send Notice of Billing Errors and Customer Service Inquiries to:
Off The Rack Credit Services
PO Box 7903828 St. Louis, MO 63179
Account Inquiries: 1-800-677-0232

Account Number: 6036 3101 9102 8828

Summary of Account Activity

Previous Balance	$238.41
Payments	- $75.00
Other Credits	- $0.00
Purchases	+ $24.83
Fees Charged	- $0.00
Interest Charged	+ $2.49
New Balance	$190.73
Past Due Amount	$0.00

Credit Limit	$500.00
Available Credit	$309.27
Statement Closing Date	10/30
Next Statement Closing Date	11/30
Days in Billing Cycle	30
Interest Charged	+ $2.49

Payment Information

New Balance	$190.73
Minimum Payment Due	$40.00
Payment Due Date	November 10

Late Payment Warning: If we do not receive your minimum payment by the date listed above, you may have to pay a late fee up to $35.

Minimum Payment Warning: If you make only the minimum payment each period, you will pay more in interest and it will take you longer to pay off your balance. *For example:*

If you make no additional charges using this card and each month you pay...	You will pay off the balance shown on this statement in about...	And you will end up paying an estimated total of...
Only the minimum payment	6 months	$211.73

If you would like information about credit counseling services, call 1-877-337-8187

Transactions

Date	Description	Amount
10/3	Payment - THANK YOU	- $75.00
10/16	In-Store Purchase	$12.18
10/27	Online Purchase	$12.65

 Please detach this portion and return with your payment to insure proper credit. Retain upper portion for your records.

Make Checks Payable to: Off The Rack Credit Services

Account Number	Payment Due	New Balance	Past Due Amount	Minimum Payment Due	Amount Enclosed
6036 3101 9102 8828	Nov. 10	$190.73	$0.00	$40.00	$

6035320292027727000000000000081410000000102

JUANITA S. ALVAREZ
2330 E. VEGAS DR.
GLENDALE HEIGHTS, IL 60139

OFF THE RACK CREDIT SERVICES
PO BOX 182676
COLUMBUS, OH 43218-2676

Name _____

Use information from page 11 to answer the questions.

1. What is the account number on this statement?
   _____

2. How much was the in-store purchase amount for this statement?
   _____

3. When was the last payment made?
   _____

4. How much money was charged in interest?
   _____

5. What is the credit limit on this statement?
   _____

6. What is the minimum payment due?
   _____

7. How long will it take to pay off the current balance if the customer just pays the minimum payment each month?
   _____

8. When is the payment due date?
   _____

9. How much is the fee for making a late payment?
   _____

CREDIT SCORE

A **credit score** is a number that helps companies decide whether to loan money. It is based on **credit history**. A credit score helps banks and businesses know if a person is likely to pay their debts. A person's credit score can be anywhere between 300 and 850. The higher a person's score, the easier it is for them to get credit.

The most commonly used credit scoring system is Fair Isaac Corporation (FICO). **FICO** created the software system that the three major credit reporting agencies—Experian, Transunion, and Equifax—use. Banks and businesses report how you use your credit to these agencies. Then, each agency uses that information to figure out your credit score. Your score may vary a little from agency to agency.

CREDIT SCORE RATINGS

Excellent: 750 and above
Good: 700 to 749
Fair: 650 to 699
Poor: 550 to 649
Bad: 550 and below

MORE ABOUT CREDIT SCORES

There are five main factors that determine a credit score.

Payment History
Payment history is the most important factor in your credit score. It includes information about how much you owe and if you make your payments on time. It makes up 35% of your score.

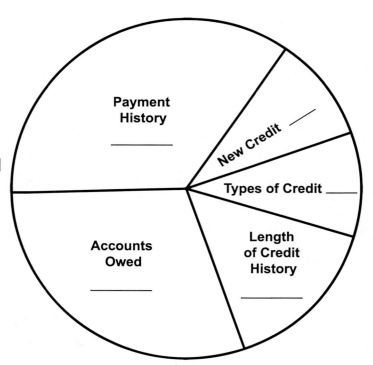

Accounts Owed
The next most important factor is the number of accounts you owe money on, the type of debt, and total amount owed. This makes up 30% of your credit score.

Length of Credit History
How long your credit accounts have been open make up 15% of your score.

Types of Credit
Another 10% of your score depends on having a variety of different kinds of accounts. If you have credit cards, make mortgage payments, and have retail accounts, it makes for a higher score.

New Credit Applications
Another 10% of your score depends on new credit applications. If you open too many new accounts in a short period of time it can lower your score.

Use the information above to add the correct percentages to the pie chart. Then, answer the following question.

Why do you think Payment History is the most important factor in a credit score?

_____
_____
_____
_____

Name _____

Use information from pages 13 and 14 to answer the questions.

1. What is a credit score?

   _____

   _____

2. How do banks and businesses use credit scores?

   _____

   _____

3. What are the three main credit reporting agencies?

   _____

   _____

4. How do the credit reporting agencies get the information to figure out a credit score?

   _____

   _____

5. What is the most important factor used in figuring out a credit score?

   _____

6. What makes up 15% of your credit score?

   _____

   _____

7. What happens if you open up too many new accounts in a short period of time?

   _____

   _____

8. If a person has a credit score of 725, what is their credit rating?

   _____

SHOULD YOU HAVE A CREDIT CARD?

Whether to get a credit card or not is a big decision. It is important to understand the advantages of having a credit card (the pros) as well as the disadvantages of having a credit card (the cons). To help with the decision, some pros and cons are listed below.

PROS	CONS
Buying on credit makes it possible to make a large purchase. You can pay the debt off in small payments over time.	If you're not careful, you can get buried in debt. You can end up buying things that you don't really need.
Carrying credit cards is easier and safer than carrying large amounts of cash. It's easier to shop with credit cards than with personal checks.	Because credit cards are so easy to use, it can also be easy to spend more than you can afford.
Some credit cards give rewards on the amount of money that you borrow. You can get a small percentage back of the money that you spend.	If you don't pay your balance off each month, you can pay a lot of extra money in interest. Sometimes you end up paying two or three times more than what the item actually costs.
Using credit responsibly builds a good credit history. This can increase your credit score. It can have a positive effect in many parts of your life.	Missing payments and going over your credit limit can ruin your credit score. This can have a negative effect in many parts of your life.

Credit Card Math RL 5.8

Name _____

Opinion: Tell what you think about using credit cards. Use information from page 16 to help answer the questions.

1. What do you think is the most important positive thing about using a credit card? Support your answer.

   _____
   _____
   _____
   _____

2. What do you think is the most important negative thing about using a credit card? Support your answer.

   _____
   _____
   _____
   _____

3. How old do you think someone should be before they are allowed to have a credit card? Support your answer.

   _____
   _____
   _____
   _____

Research: Ask 5 adults the following questions and write the number of yes answers and the number of no answers.

1. Do you use credit cards?   _____ Yes   _____ No
2. Do you think it's easy to overspend using a credit card?   _____ Yes   _____ No
3. Do you have more than 4 credit cards?   _____ Yes   _____ No
4. Do you think teenagers should have credit cards?   _____ Yes   _____ No

Name _____

REVIEW
PRE-/POST-TEST

Shade in the letter next to the correct answer.

1. The microchip on the front of a credit card
   - Ⓐ replaces the account number.
   - Ⓑ is for extra security and to prevent fraud.
   - Ⓒ tells what kind of card it is.
   - Ⓓ none of the above

2. You do not have to pay interest on your debt if you pay off the balance within
   - Ⓐ 5 to 10 days.
   - Ⓑ 3 to 6 months.
   - Ⓒ 25 to 30 days.
   - Ⓓ 1 to 2 years.

3. Visa and MasterCard are companies that
   - Ⓐ process credit card payments between banks and merchants.
   - Ⓑ give out most of the credit cards.
   - Ⓒ figure out your credit score.
   - Ⓓ set your credit limit.

4. What is the main factor in figuring out a credit score?
   - Ⓐ how much money you make
   - Ⓑ your payment history
   - Ⓒ the number of times you have applied for credit
   - Ⓓ how long you have had a credit card

5. To get a student credit card, you must
   - Ⓐ be at least 18 years old.
   - Ⓑ have graduated from high school.
   - Ⓒ get good grades in college.
   - Ⓓ have someone who can pay for the card.

6. How is a secured credit card different from other types of credit cards?
   - Ⓐ You can only use it to buy certain types of things.
   - Ⓑ You must have good credit to get one.
   - Ⓒ You must have a co-signer on the account.
   - Ⓓ You must give a cash deposit to cover your credit limit.

7. A credit score of 685 is considered
   - Ⓐ excellent.
   - Ⓑ fair.
   - Ⓒ poor.
   - Ⓓ good.

8. What might happen if you don't make your credit card payment by the due date?
   - Ⓐ Your card will be canceled.
   - Ⓑ You will not be able to get another credit card.
   - Ⓒ You will have to pay a late fee.
   - Ⓓ none of the above

Credit Card Math

FACT SHEET #1

Peter B. Chen

Birthday April 14, 1986
Social Security 685-22-3410

Home Information

Current Address	**Previous Address**
4622 Woodlawan Ave. N.	3700 Beach Drive S.W. #334
Seattle, WA 98103	Seattle, WA 98116
Peter owns this house.	*Peter rented this apartment.*
He has lived here for 5 years and 6 months.	*He lived there for 8 years and 2 months.*

Cell Phone 206-322-9765   **Email** pbchen@gmail.com

Employment Information

Employer	Postion		Gross Monthly Income
REI	Store Manager	6 Years / 4 Months	$4,950.00
222 Yale Av. N.			
Seattle, WA 98109			
206-223-1944			

Other Income Source
Rowing Instructor   Teaches beginning rowing lessons at Lake Union on the weekends.
Monthly Income: $450.00

Credit References

Bank of Seattle	Checking Account Number:	68843339
Northwest Credit Union	Savings Account Number:	99900321
Mortgage		Monthly Payment: $2,275.00

Creditors

Hal's Men's Shop	Peter Owes: $1,350.00	Monthly Payment: $52.00
American Express	Peter Owes: $3,400.00	Monthly Payment: $154.00

©Remedia Publications   *Credit Card Math*

Name _____

Use information from page 19 to fill out the application form.

Century Bank — CREDIT CARD APPLICATION

APPLICANT INFORMATION		
LAST NAME	FIRST NAME MI	BIRTH DATE
SOCIAL SECURITY NO.	TELEPHONE	
CURRENT ADDRESS APT. NO.		HOW LONG? ____Yrs. ____Months ☐ Rent ☐ Own ☐ Live with Others
CITY / STATE / ZIP		
PREVIOUS ADDRESS APT. NO.		HOW LONG? ____Yrs. ____Months ☐ Rent ☐ Own ☐ Live with Others
CITY / STATE / ZIP		

EMPLOYMENT INFORMATION		
CURRENT EMPLOYER	POSITION	____ Yrs. ____ Mos.
STREET ADDRESS		PHONE NUMBER
CITY / STATE / ZIP		GROSS MONTHLY INCOME
OTHER INCOME SOURCE	MONTHLY AMOUNT	

CREDIT REFERENCES	
CHECKING ACCOUNT BANK	SAVINGS ACCOUNT BANK
ACCOUNT NO.	ACCOUNT NO.
LANDLORD'S NAME *(if renting)*	MONTHLY RENT OR MORTGAGE

NAMES OF CREDITORS	AMOUNT OWED	MONTHLY PAYMENT

Credit Card Math ©Remedia Publications

Name _____

Peter Chen was approved for a credit card from Century Bank. His credit limit is $4,300.00.

Use information from page 19 and Peter's credit card to answer the following questions and solve the word problems.

Century **Bank**

159 2449 9654 8001

Good Thru 09/24

PETER B. CHEN

1. What is Peter's total monthly income? _____

2. What is the total of Peter's monthly payments to creditors? _____

3. After making his monthly credit payments and mortgage payment each month, how much does Peter have left over from his total monthly income? _____

4. When does Peter's new credit card expire? _____

5. What is Peter's account number? _____

6. Peter is thinking about buying a wooden rowboat for $1,943.00. His monthly payment for the boat will be $147.00.

   If he buys the rowboat, what will his total debt be, including what he owes his current creditors? _____

   What will his total monthly credit payments be, including payments to his current creditors? _____

©Remedia Publications   21   *Credit Card Math*

Name _____

Remember, Peter's credit limit is $4,300.00. Use this information to solve the word problems.

1. Peter's first purchase with his new credit card was at Larsen's Department Store. He bought a pair of shoes for $34.95, a pair of jeans for $64.50, and sweatshirt for $24.99.

   What is the total for Peter's purchases? _____

   How much of Peter's credit limit is left? _____

2. Peter purchased a roundtrip airline ticket from Seattle to Dallas online. He paid $648.00 for his ticket, $25.00 to check his bag, and $35.00 to upgrade his seat.

   What was his total cost for flying to Dallas? _____

   How much of Peter's credit is left after this purchase? _____

Use Peter's credit card to fill out the form to complete his online transaction.

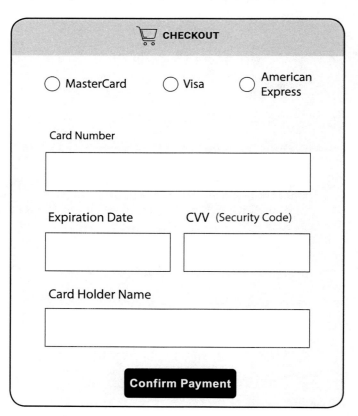

Credit Card Math

Century Bank

ACCOUNT STATEMENT

Balance Summary

Previous Balance	$124.44
Payments	− $50.00
Other Credits	− $0.00
Cash Advances	+ $0.00
New Purchases	+ $808.48
Fees Charged	**+ $0.00**
Interest Charged	**+ $2.39**
New Balance	= $885.31

Total Credit Limit $4,300

Peter Chen
Account Number 159 2449 9654 8001
Statement Billing Period 3/1 to 4/1

24-Hour Customer Service 1-800-555-4701
TTY for Hearing/Speech Imparied: 1-800-555-4740
Outside the US Call Collect: 1-925-555-4744
Gold Standard Bank Online: goldstandarbank.com

Send General Inquiries To:
PO Box 10000, Des Moines IA, 50306-0347

Total Available Credit $3,414.69

Payment Information

New Balance	$885.31
Minimum Payment	$75.00
Payment Due Date	04/25

Late Payment Warning: If we do not receive your minimum payment by the date listed above, you may have to pay a late fee up to $35.

Transactions

Date	Reference	Description	Credits	Charges
Payments				
3/15	ONLINE	PAYMENT	$50.00	
Purchases				
3/10	ONLINE	WESTERN AIRLINES		$708.00
3/18	ONLINE	EBAY		$18.85
3/12	IN-STORE	MATT'S DINER		$42.98
3/27	IN-STORE	5 STAR SPORTS		$38.65
		TOTAL NEW PURCHASES		$808.48

©Remedia Publications   *Credit Card Math*

Name _____

Use information from pages 19 and 23 to answer the questions.

1. What is the total for online purchases? _____

2. What is the total for in-store purchases? _____

3. How much more was spent online than in-store? _____

4. How much is the minimum payment due and when is the due date? _____

5. If Peter makes the minimum payment, what will his total credit payments be for this month? Include his other monthly payments to creditors. _____

6. How much interest did Peter pay? _____

7. How much is Peter's available credit? _____

8. What is the new balance on the credit card? _____

9. If Peter makes a payment of $187.00, what will the new balance be? _____

10. What will Peter's available credit be after he makes a payment of $187.00? _____

Credit Card Math

Name _____

A line graph shows information with a line drawn from one point to another. It is usually used to show how something has changed over time.

Last year, Peter's credit score changed every month. Use the information from the chart to the right to complete the line graph. Draw a solid line.

LAST YEAR	
January	690
February	720
March	650
April	700
May	725
June	650
July	700
August	740

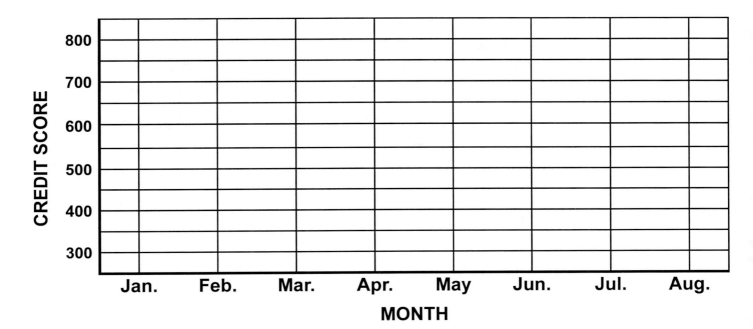

Compare last year's credit score to this year. On the same line graph, add the data from the chart to the right using a broken line. This will show how Peter's credit score changed for the same time period in this year.

THIS YEAR	
January	625
February	650
March	675
April	725
May	750
June	690
July	750
August	700

Overall, which do you think was Peter's best year for his credit score? Support your answer.

_____
_____
_____

FACT SHEET #2

Keisha V. Reynolds

Birthday December 10, 1994
Social Security 323-56-7844

Home Information

Current Address
65 Bennington Place #405
Deerfield, IL 60015
Keisha rents this apartment.
She has lived here for 2 years, 3 month.

Previous Address
783 Windham St. #708
Deerfield, IL 60015
Keisha rented this apartment.
She lived there for 1 year, 5 months.

Cell Phone 847-555-9219

Email KeishaR@windsorpub.com

Employment Information

Employer	Postion		Gross Monthly Income
Windsor Publishing 664 N. 39th. St. Chicago, IL 60611 847-555-6821	Assistant Editor	2 years / 6 months	$3,250.00

Other Income Source
English Tutor   Monthly Income: $525.00

Credit References

Valley Bank	Checking Account Number:	9866523
Valley Bank	Savings Account Number:	9866524
Landlord: Wendy Blake		Monthly Rent: $1,250.00

Creditors

Valley Bank MasterCard®	Keisha Owes $2,554.89	Monthly Payment: $94.00
Target	Keisha Owes $345.00	Monthly Payment: $25.00

Credit Card Math   ©Remedia Publications

Name _____

Use information from page 26 to fill out the application form.

Liberty DEPARTMENT STORE — CREDIT CARD APPLICATION

APPLICANT INFORMATION			
LAST NAME	FIRST NAME	MI	BIRTH DATE
SOCIAL SECURITY NO.		TELEPHONE	
CURRENT ADDRESS		APT. NO.	HOW LONG? ____Yrs. ____Months
CITY / STATE / ZIP			☐ Rent ☐ Own ☐ Live with Others
PREVIOUS ADDRESS		APT. NO.	HOW LONG? ____Yrs. ____Months
CITY / STATE / ZIP			☐ Rent ☐ Own ☐ Live with Others

EMPLOYMENT INFORMATION		
CURRENT EMPLOYER	POSITION	____ Yrs. ____ Mos.
STREET ADDRESS	PHONE NUMBER	
CITY / STATE / ZIP	GROSS MONTHLY INCOME	
OTHER INCOME SOURCE	MONTHLY AMOUNT	

CREDIT REFERENCES	
<u>CHECKING ACCOUNT</u> BANK	<u>SAVINGS ACCOUNT</u> BANK
ACCOUNT NO.	ACCOUNT NO.
LANDLORD'S NAME *(if renting)*	MONTHLY RENT OR MORTGAGE

NAMES OF CREDITORS	AMOUNT OWED	MONTHLY PAYMENT

Credit Card Math

Name _____

Keisha Reynolds was approved for a credit card from Liberty Department Store. Her credit limit is $1,550.00.

Use information from page 26 and Keisha's credit card to answer the following questions and solve the word problems.

Liberty

279 9811 0291 7753

Good Thru **10/26**

KEISHA REYNOLDS

1. What is Keisha's account number? _____

2. How much does Keisha make each month as an English tutor? _____

3. What is Keisha's total monthly income? _____

4. How much is the total amount that Keisha owes on her two credit cards? _____

5. After Keisha pays her rent and her two credit card payments, how much does she have left from her total monthly income? _____

6. When does Keisha's new credit card expire? _____

7. How much more does Keisha owe on her Valley Bank MasterCard® than on her Target card? _____

8. If Keisha purchases a pair of shoes for $53.69 and a jacket for $137.29 from Liberty Department store, how much of her credit limit will be left? _____

Credit Card Math

Name _____

Below are images of Keisha's three credit cards. Use the information from these cards and and from page 26 to answer the following questions and solve the word problems.

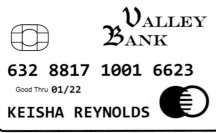
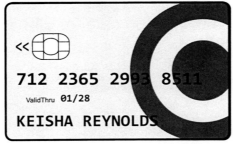

Credit Limit $3,275.00   **Credit Limit $1,225.00**   **Credit Limit $1,550.00**

1. Based on what Keisha owes on her Valley Bank MasterCard®, what is her available credit on this card? _____

2. Including all three credit cards, how much total credit does Keisha have? _____

3. After deducting how much Keisha owes on her Valley Bank card and her Target card, how much is Keisha's total available credit on these two cards? _____

4. Keisha wants to buy a train ticket for $89.00. Which credit card should she use? Explain why.

   _____

   _____

5. Which of these credit cards will expire first? _____

Name _____

Use information from page 26 to answer the questions.

1. Keisha was excited to use her Liberty credit card. She went shopping on Saturday afternoon. She needed some things for a beach vacation. She bought three pairs of flip flops for $19.99 each, two pairs of sunglasses for $15.69 each, and four T-shirts that were on sale for $12.59 each.

   How much did Keisha spend for her
   beach vacation? _____

2. Keisha and a friend went on vacation. Keisha used her credit card to pay the hotel bill. The amount owed was $640.86.

   How much was each girl's share? _____

3. Keisha is paid twice each month. She sets aside money from each pay check for her monthly payments to Valley Bank and Target.

   How much money will she need from each
   paycheck to make these payments? _____

4. Keisha got a new catalog in the mail. Use information from page 26 and her credit card to fill in the form. She will need this information to place her order.

SHIPPING ADDRESS	CREDIT CARD NUMBER	
	EXPIRATION DATE	SECURITY CODE
CITY	STATE	CARD HOLDER'S NAME
ZIP CODE	PHONE NUMBER	

Credit Card Math — 30 — ©Remedia Publications

Name _____

Use the following information to fill in the blanks on Keisha's Liberty Department Store account statement on page 32. Write the information in the correct boxes.

- The previous balance is $385.32

- The last payment amount is $58.00

- There were no credits, cash advances, or fees charged.

- She was charged $4.85 in interest.

- The minimum payment due is $64.00.

- Her total Credit Limit is $1,550.00.

- The payment due date is 10/28.

- In-store purchases include: a handbag for $43.95 on 9/10, a scarf for $16.39 on 9/15, a pair of jeans for $64.45 on 9/18

- Online purchases include: a sun hat for $24.95 on 9/5, a pair of shorts for $33.50 on 9/25

Use the information above to solve the following word problems. Finish filling in the blanks on Keisha's account statement with the answers for questions 3, 4, and 5.

1. How much did Keisha spend for online purchases? _____

2. How much did Keisha spend for in-store purchases? _____

3. What is the total for all of Keisha's purchases for this billing period? _____

4. How much is Keisha's new balance? _____

5. How much is Keisha's available credit? _____

©Remedia Publications   *Credit Card Math*

Liberty DEPARTMENT STORE
ACCOUNT STATEMENT

Balance Summary

Previous Balance	
Payments	−
Other Credits	−
Cash Advances	+
New Purchases	+
Fees Charged	+
Interest Charged	+
New Balance	=

Keisha Reynolds
Account Number 279 9811 0291 7753
Statement Billing Period 9/1 to 10/1

24-Hour Customer Service 1-800-555-4701
TTY for Hearing/Speech Imparied: 1-800-555-4990
Outside the US Call Collect: 1-925-555-4994
Gold Standard Bank Online: libertydepartmentstore.com

Send General Inquiries To:
PO BOX 50000, CHICAGO, IL, 60007-0347

Total Credit Limit [ ]   Total Available Credit [ ]

Payment Information

New Balance	
Minimum Payment	
Payment Due Date	

Late Payment Warning: If we do not receive your minimum payment by the date listed above, you may have to pay a late fee up to $35.

Transactions

Date	Reference	Description	Charges
NONE			

Purchases

Trans	Refernce	Description	Charges
9/5	ONLINE		
9/25	ONLINE		
9/10	IN-STORE		
9/15	IN-STORE		
9/18	IN-STORE		
		TOTAL NEW PURCHASES	

Credit Card Math ©Remedia Publications

Name _____

A bar graph uses horizontal or vertical bars to show how things compare to one another. It can also show how something has changed over time.

CREDIT SCORES	
January	700
February	725
March	800
April	750
May	750
June	700
July	650
August	725

For the past 8 months, Keisha's credit score has changed every month. Use the information from the chart to the right to complete the bar graph about Keisha's monthly credit score.

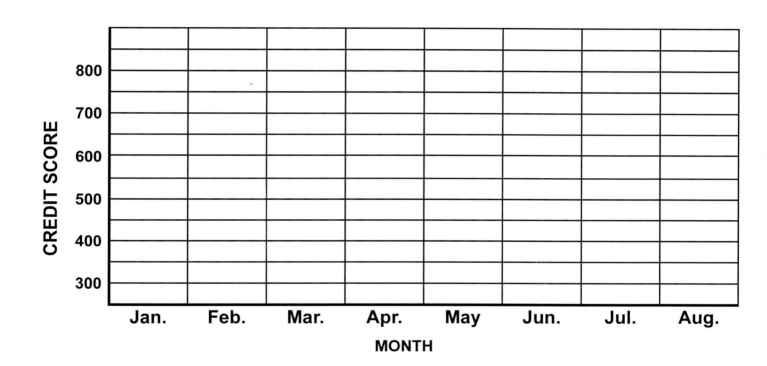

1. How many months did Keisha have a credit score of 725 or higher? _____

2. How many months did Keisha have a credit score lower than 700? _____

3. What was Keisha's average credit score over the past 8 months? _____

©Remedia Publications   33   *Credit Card Math*

FACT SHEET #3

Alex C. Bailey

Birthday August 14, 1996
Social Security 642-89-7624

Home Information

Current Address	**Previous Address**
678 Birch St. #512	344 N. Berkeley St.
Greensboro, NC 27405	Boston, MA 02116
Alex rents this apartment.	*Alex rented this house.*
He has lived there for 1 year, 8 months.	*He lived there for 2 years, 6 month.*

Cell Phone 336-555-8734   **Email** ACB@yahoo.com

Employment Information

Employer   Postion   Gross Monthly Income
Big T Sporting Goods   Shipping Clerk   1 year / 7 months $2,800.00
1203 Industrial Way
Greensboro, NC 27406
336-555-2289

Other Income Source
Personal Trainer   Monthly Income: $672.00

Credit References

Old South Bank   Checking Account Number: 5778326

Old South Bank   Savings Account Number: 5778337

Landlord: George Pickett   Monthly Rent: $1,100.00

Creditors

Bayside Subaru   Alex Owes $12,849.20   Monthly Payment: $258.65

Home Store   Alex Owes $668.45   Monthly Payment: $72.39

Credit Card Math   ©Remedia Publications

Name _____

Use information from page 34 to fill out the application form

TRINITY BANK — CREDIT CARD APPLICATION

APPLICANT INFORMATION

LAST NAME	FIRST NAME	MI	BIRTH DATE

SOCIAL SECURITY NO.	TELEPHONE

CURRENT ADDRESS	APT. NO.	HOW LONG? ____Yrs. ____Months ☐Rent ☐Own ☐Live with Others
CITY / STATE / ZIP		

PREVIOUS ADDRESS	APT. NO.	HOW LONG? ____Yrs. ____Months ☐Rent ☐Own ☐Live with Others
CITY / STATE / ZIP		

EMPLOYMENT INFORMATION

CURRENT EMPLOYER	POSITION	____ Yrs. ____ Mos.
STREET ADDRESS	PHONE NUMBER	
CITY / STATE / ZIP	GROSS MONTHLY INCOME	
OTHER INCOME SOURCE	MONTHLY AMOUNT	

CREDIT REFERENCES

CHECKING ACCOUNT BANK	SAVINGS ACCOUNT BANK
ACCOUNT NO.	ACCOUNT NO.

LANDLORD'S NAME *(if renting)*	MONTHLY RENT OR MORTGAGE

NAMES OF CREDITORS	AMOUNT OWED	MONTHLY PAYMENT

Name _____

Alex Bailey was approved for a credit card from Trinity Bank. His credit limit is $3,450.00.

Use information from page 34 and Alex's credit card to answer the following questions and solve the word problems.

TRINITY BANK

879 3485 8124 0035

Good Thru 12/26

ALEX C. BAILEY   VISA

1. How much is Alex's total monthly income?   _____

2. How much is Alex's total weekly income?   _____

3. What is Alex's total income for a year?   _____

4. If Alex charges $896.39 on his new credit card the first month, how much available credit will he have?   _____

5. When does Alex's new credit card expire?   _____

6. How much longer did Alex live at his previous address than he has lived at his current address?   _____

7. If Alex makes six payments on his Subaru, what is the total amount that he will pay?   _____

8. How much will Alex pay in rent for a year?   _____

Credit Card Math   ©Remedia Publications

Name _____

Use information from page 34 to answer the questions.

1. Alex used his Trinity Visa® card to take advantage of a sale on bath towels. He bought eight towels for a total of $68.00.

   What was the cost per towel? _____

2. If Alex doubles his Subaru payments each month for a year, what is the total amount he will pay? _____

3. Alex's credit limit at the Home Store is $1,250.00. Based on what he currently owes how much is his available credit? _____

SAVE 45% — **STEWART'S sporting goods**

Present this coupon at checkout to receive 45% off your purchase of $100.00 or more. Offer expires December 31.

4. Stewart's Sporting Goods is having a 45% off sale. Alex used his Trinity Visa® card card to buy a rain jacket that regularly cost $56.00 and a pair of ski pants that regularly cost $129.00.

   With the 45% discount, how much did Alex spend? _____

   How much was Alex's total savings? _____

5. Alex spent $1,152.00 the first year he used his Trinity Visa Credit Card. What was the average amount he spent each month? _____

6. For a limited time, Trinity Bank is offering 3% cash back on monthly purchases (3% of the total purchase). Alex spent $465.00 last month.

   How much cash back will Alex get? _____

©Remedia Publications — *Credit Card Math*

Alex needs some things to fix up his apartment. He went to the Home Store website to do some shopping.

Name _____

Use information from page 38 to answer the questions.

1. Which of the lamps shown offers the
   biggest savings? _____

2. Alex bought two Mid-Century Modern Lamps and
   one Brass Lamp. How much did Alex spend
   on lamps? _____

   How much was his total savings? _____

Home store — **SAVE 35% on Pillows**
Online orders: include coupon code **SAVE35** at checkout to receive
35% off your purchase of $50.00 or more. Offer expires July 31.

----

3. Alex needed some new pillows for his couch. He bought four Zig Zag pillows.
   He used a 35% off coupon on the pillows.

   How much did Alex spend on the pillows? _____

   With the coupon, how much did Alex save? _____

4. The Multi-Color cups come in a set of six. The other cups are sold individually.

   What is the price per cup of the Multi-Color cups? _____

   How much would a set of six Polka Dot Fantasy
   cups cost? _____

5. Alex bought five Cobalt Blue cups. How much did
   he spend on the cups? _____

Name _____

Use your answers about Alex's Home Store purchases on page 39 to solve the following word problems. Round your answers to the nearest hundredths place if needed.

1. What is the subtotal for Alex's online purchases? _____

2. Sales tax on the purchase is 8%. How much did Alex spend in sales tax? _____

3. It will cost $15.49 to ship Alex's order. Including sales tax and shipping, what is the total that will be charged to his Home Store account? _____

Fill in the blanks of this online order form using the answers to the questions above and on page 39.

http://shop-home-store.com

Home store — CHECKOUT

YOUR CART   SHIPPING INFO   PAYMENT

ITEM	UNIT PRICE		QTY	PRICE
Mid-Century Modern Lamp	$28.50		2	
Brass Lamp	$21.00		1	
Zig Zag Pillow	$16.50	Minus 35% Discount	4	
Cobalt Blue Cup	$9.50		5	
			Subtotal	_____
			Sales Tax	_____
			Shipping	_____
			Total	_____

Credit Card Math   ©Remedia Publications

Name _____

Use information from page 34 and Alex's Home Store credit card to fill in the blanks to finish this online order.

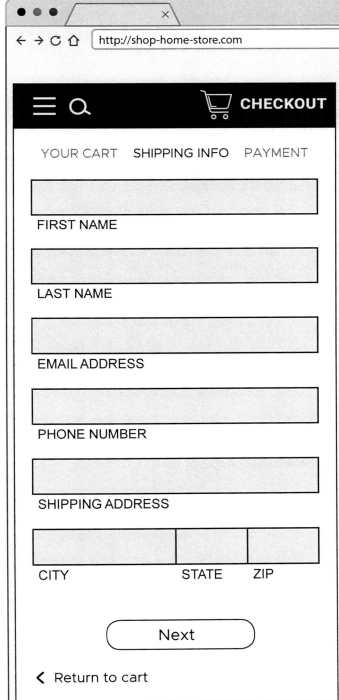

FACT SHEET #4

Carmela D. Martinez

Birthday February 9, 1984
Social Security 433-96-0031

Home Information

Current Address
1631 Orange Blossom Lane
Anaheim, CA 92801
Carmela owns this house.
She has lived there for 10 years, 4 months.

Previous Address
3310 Oak Blvd.
Houston, TX 77056
Carmela rented this house.
She lived there for 4 years, 10 months.

Cell Phone 714-555-9063   **Email** carmeladm@gmail.com

Employment Information

Employer	Postion		Gross Monthly Income
Citex Corporation 821 Lindsey Way Anaheim, CA 92801 714-555-1589	Marketing Manager	8 years / 5 months	$7,080.00

Credit References

Bristol Bank	Checking Account Number:	3216455
Bristol Bank	Savings Account Number:	3216466
Mortgage		Monthly Payment: $2,890.00

Creditors

Marks Chevrolet	Carmela Owes $18,643.59	Monthly Payment: $296.42
Star Bank Visa®	Carmela Owes $2,650.86	Monthly Payment: $142.90
Macy's	Carmela Owes $849.38	Monthly Payment: $85.40

Credit Card Math   ©Remedia Publications

Name _____

Use information from page 42 to fill out the application form.

WESTERN STATES BANK — CREDIT CARD APPLICATION

APPLICANT INFORMATION

LAST NAME	FIRST NAME	MI	BIRTH DATE
SOCIAL SECURITY NO.		TELEPHONE	
CURRENT ADDRESS		APT. NO.	HOW LONG? ____Yrs. ____Months ☐Rent ☐Own ☐Live with Others
CITY / STATE / ZIP			
PREVIOUS ADDRESS		APT. NO.	HOW LONG? ____Yrs. ____Months ☐Rent ☐Own ☐Live with Others
CITY / STATE / ZIP			

EMPLOYMENT INFORMATION

CURRENT EMPLOYER	POSITION	____ Yrs. ____ Mos.
STREET ADDRESS	PHONE NUMBER	
CITY / STATE / ZIP	GROSS MONTHLY INCOME	
OTHER INCOME SOURCE	MONTHLY AMOUNT	

CREDIT REFERENCES

CHECKING ACCOUNT BANK	SAVINGS ACCOUNT BANK
ACCOUNT NO.	ACCOUNT NO.
LANDLORD'S NAME *(if renting)*	MONTHLY RENT OR MORTGAGE

NAMES OF CREDITORS	AMOUNT OWED	MONTHLY PAYMENT

©Remedia Publications · Credit Card Math

Name _____

Use information from page 42 to answer the questions.

1. How much longer has Carmela lived at her current address than she did at her previous address? _____

2. How much is Carmela's income for a year? _____

3. How much does Carmela make per week? _____

4. What does Carmela spend each month to pay her mortgage and her creditors? _____

5. How much of her gross monthly income is left after she makes all her monthly payments? _____

6. What is the total amount of Carmela's debt? Include what she owes on her car, her Star Bank Visa®, and her Macy's account. _____

7. If Carmela doubled her car payments for a year, how much will she have paid toward her car loan? _____

   What would the new balance on her car be? _____

Name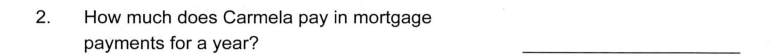

Use information from page 42 to answer the questions.

1. If Carmela was saving weekly to make her monthly mortgage payment, how much will she need to save per week? _____

2. How much does Carmela pay in mortgage payments for a year? _____

3. Carmela's monthly mortgage payment includes property taxes and homeowner's insurance. 8% of the monthly payment goes toward property taxes. 3% of the monthly payment goes towards homeowner's insurance.

    How much of the monthly payment goes towards property taxes? _____

    How much of the monthly payment goes towards homeowner's insurance? _____

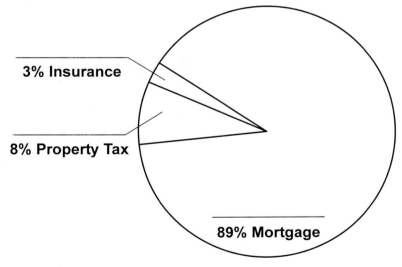

Fill in the blanks on this pie chart to show Carmela's monthly mortgage payment.

4. How much does Carmela pay in property taxes per year? _____

5. How much does Carmela pay in homeowner's insurance per year? _____

Name _____

Carmela was approved for her Western States MasterCard®. Since her credit score is 825, the bank gave her a credit limit of $8,500.00.
Answer the following questions and solve the word problems. Round your answers to the nearest hundredths place if needed.

```
WESTERN STATES BANK
731 1200 0381 1459
Valid Thru 03/22
CARMELA D. MARTINEZ
109
```

1. Use the Western States MasterCard® to answer the following questions. What is Carmela's account number? _____

    When is the card's expiration date? _____

    What is the security code? _____

2. To celebrate getting her new credit card, Carmela and four friends went out to lunch. They ordered five salads at $16.45 each. They each had an iced tea at $2.25 per glass. Everyone had chocolate cake for dessert. The dessert total was $26.25.

    What was their total for lunch? _____

    How much was each dessert? _____

    The sales tax for the meal is 8% of the total. How much is the sales tax? _____

    They added a 20% tip to the lunch total before tax. How much is the tip? _____

    Including tax and tip how much is the total bill? _____

    Carmela is going to charge 1/3 of the bill on her new card? How much will she pay? _____

Credit Card Math 46 ©Remedia Publications

Carmela wants to use her new Western States MasterCard® to buy some electronic devices. She went to the Tech World website to do some online shopping.

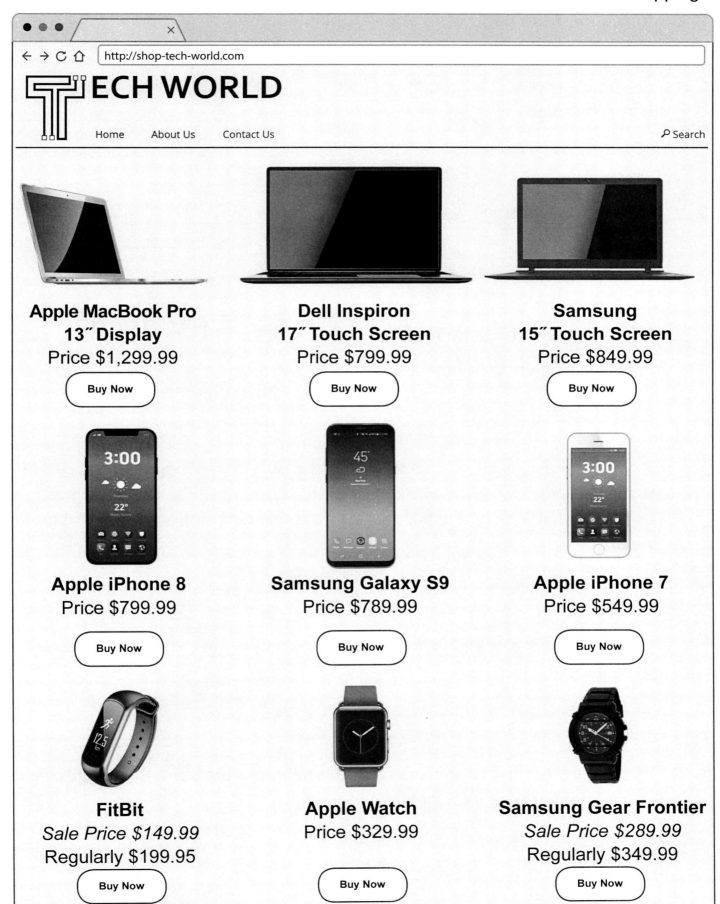

Name _____

Use information from page 47 to answer the questions.

1. How much more is a MacBook Pro than a Samsung laptop? _____

2. If Carmela buys three iPhone 8s for her family, how much will she spend? _____

3. Which of the two smart watches on sale offer the biggest savings? _____

   What is the difference in the savings amount? _____

**Buy 2 or More Online &
SAVE 15%
On Apple Products**

TECH WORLD

Save 15% on Apple products when you buy two or more. Online offer only limited to stock on hand. Cannot be combined with any other discounts. Offer expires May 25.
Use Coupon Code APPLE15.

---

4. Carmela got a 15% off coupon for Apple products in an email. She decided to use the coupon for part of her purchase. She bought an iPhone 7 for herself, her husband, her mom and her brother. She also bought a MacBook Pro for herself.

   How much did she spend on the iPhones with the discount? _____

   How much did she spend on the MacBook Pro with the discount? _____

   With the discount how much was her total savings on Apple products? _____

5. Carmela and her husband just started a new fitness program. She bought them each a Fit Bit to keep track of their progress.

   How much did she spend on the Fit Bits? _____

   How much did she save on her purchase? _____

Credit Card Math

Name _____

Use your answers from page 48 to solve the word problems. Round your answers to the nearest hundredths place if needed.

1. What is the subtotal for Carmela's online purchases? _____

2. Sales tax on the purchase is 7%. How much did Carmela spend on sales tax? _____

3. It will cost $16.48 to ship Carmela's order express. Including sales tax and shipping, what is the total that be charged to her Western States credit card? _____

Fill in the blanks of this online order form using the answers to the questions above and on page 48.

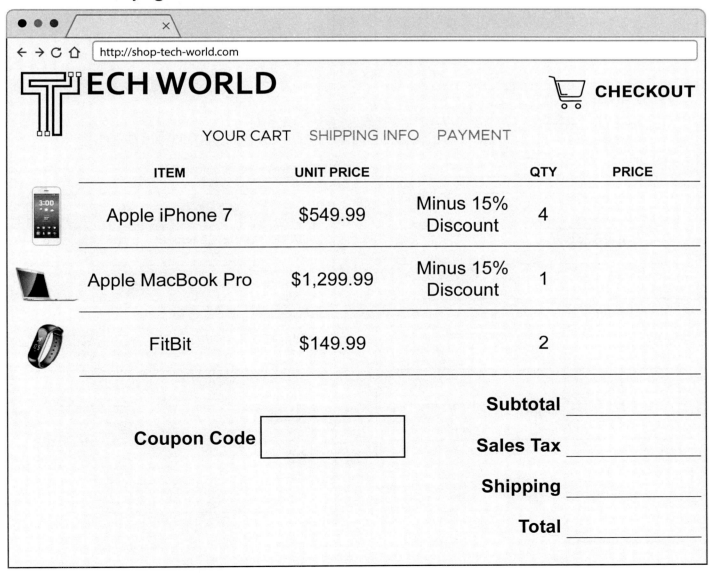

Name _____

Use information from page 42 and and Carmela's Western States MasterCard® to fill in the blanks and finish this online order.

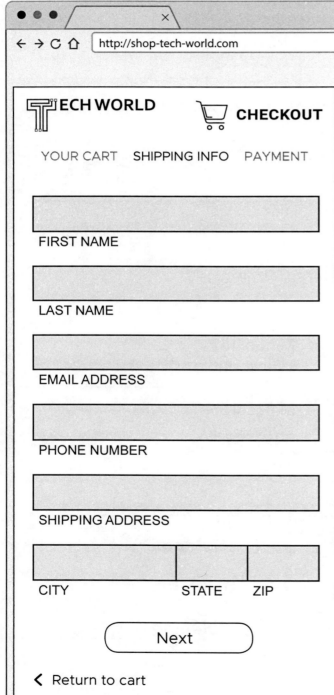

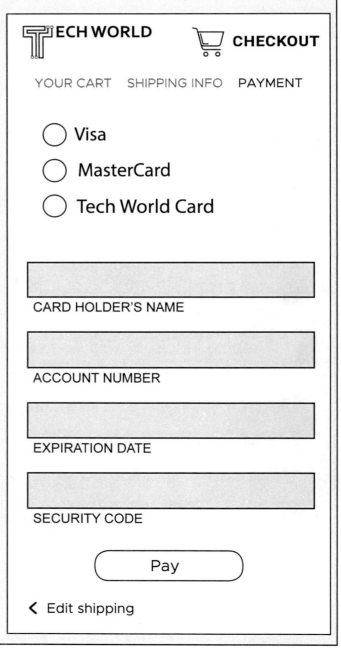

Name _____

You have just been approved for a Visa® card from Zenith Bank! Your credit limit is $500.00.

Print your name on the front of the card and sign your name on the back. Now it's ready to use. Shop online at the website below for some fun sports products.

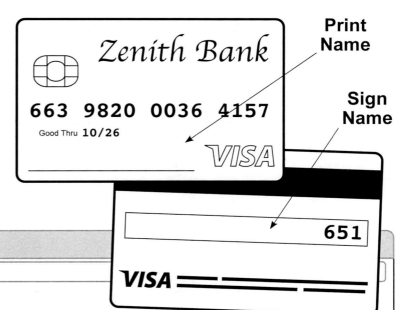

http://shop-stewarts-sporting-goods.com

STEWART'S sporting goods

Home   About Us   Contact Us   🔍 Search

Inline Skates
Price $64.99

Buy Now

37" Skateboard
Price $34.99

Buy Now

Tennis Racquet
Price $29.97

Buy Now

Power Jump Trampoline
Price $249.95

Buy Now

Frisbee Golf Set of 5
Price $39.98

Buy Now

Mountain Bike
Price $299.98

Buy Now

©Remedia Publications — Credit Card Math

Name _____

Use information from page 51 to complete the order form below. Choose two or three products from the website using your Zenith credit card.

- List the products on the form.

- Write the name of each item, the unit price, the quantity and the total price.

- Add up the amount of your purchase and write the answer on the Subtotal line.

- The sales tax is 8%. Figure out the tax on your purchase and write the answer on the Sales Tax line.

- Shipping is free for this purchase.

- Add the Subtotal to the Sales tax for the total of your purchase. Write the answer on the Total line.

How much of your credit limit is left after you make this purchase? _____

http://shop-stewarts-sporting-goods.com

STEWART'S sporting goods

YOUR CART   SHIPPING INFO   PAYMENT   **CHECKOUT**

ITEM	UNIT PRICE	QTY	PRICE

Subtotal _____
Sales Tax _____
Shipping _____
Total _____

Credit Card Math   52   ©Remedia Publications

Name _____

Fill in the shipping information form with your own information. Use your Zenith credit card to fill in the payment form to complete your order and checkout.

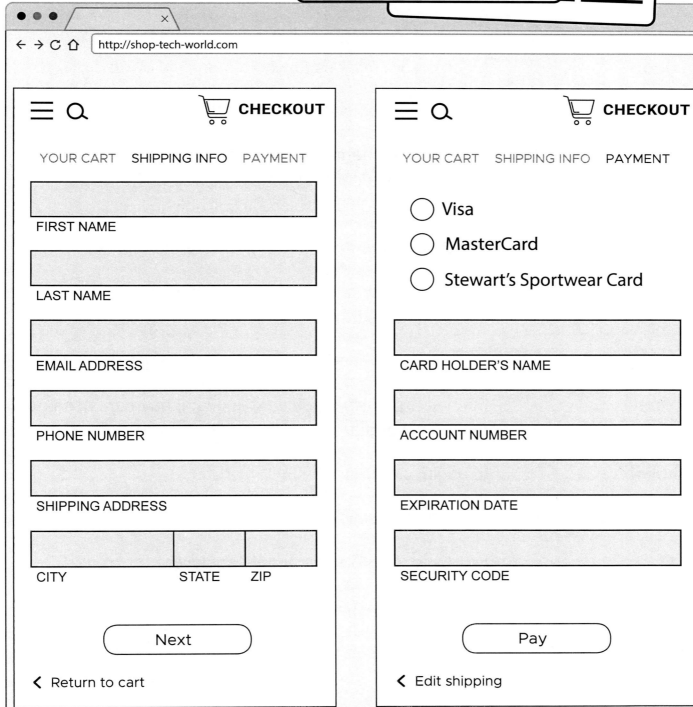

GLOSSARY

authorized	to be officially approved
account number	unique number given to a credit card customer; the number is usually embossed on the front of the credit card
balance	the amount owed
debt	an amount of money that is owed to another person, bank or business
creditor	a person or business to whom money is owed
credit history	a record of a person's debt
credit card machine	a device merchants use to process credit cards; the machine has a card reader that can read the magentic stripe or microchip on a credit card
credit limit	maximum amount a person may charge on a credit card
credit reference	information given by a person or a business about how someone uses their credit
credit score	a number that shows how creditworthy a person is
due date	the date by which a payment is due; if payment does not arrive by that date, a late fee will be charged
establish	to begin, create or set up
expiration date	the date until which you can use something
FICO	Fair Isaac Corporation; a data analytics company
fraud	the tricking of someone in order to cheat
gross monthly income	Total amount earned before any tax deductions
interest	a percentage of money that is owed on top of money borrowed

GLOSSARY

late fee	the amount of money added if a payment is not made on time
lender	a person, bank, or business that loans money
magnetic stripe	a black, brown, or silver strip of magnetic information found on the back of a credit card
MasterCard®	a company that processes credit card transactions
merchant	a person or business that sells goods for profit
microchip	a small, thin piece of material with tiny electronic parts
minimum payment	lowest amount of money customer is required to pay
NFC	near field communication; wireless technology that lets two devices communicate and share data
primary	first or main
RFID	radio frequency identification; sends very short radio signals
security	protection from harm or loss
security code	a three- to four-digit number often printed on the back of a credit card
software	programs that a computer uses to perform tasks
subtotal	the sales amount before taxes, shipping, or discounts are applied to an order
transaction	a business exchange between a cardholder and a merchant
Visa®	a company that processes credit card transactions

Name _____

GLOSSARY MATCH-UP

Choose the word or phrase from the word box that matches each definition. Write it on the blank line.

expiration date	lender	late fee	debt
credit score	interest	balance	credit reference

1. the amount of money owed on a credit card after the last payment _____

2. a number that shows if a person has good credit _____

3. extra money that you owe on top of what you borrow _____

4. the date until which you can use something _____

5. person, bank, or business that loans money _____

6. an amount of money owed to a business or bank _____

7. a charge added to a bill if a payment is not made on time _____

8. information about how a person uses their credit _____

Name _____ GLOSSARY MATCH-UP

Choose the word or phrase from the word box that matches each definition. Write it on the blank line.

microchip	merchant	fraud
transaction	available credit	minimum payment
security code	credit history	

1. a business exchange _____

2. a person or business that sells products _____

3. the amount of credit you have left to spend _____

4. the lowest amount you are required to pay on a bill _____

5. a small, thin piece of material on the front of a credit card _____

6. a record of a person's debt _____

7. a three-digit number on the back of a credit card _____

8. tricking someone in order to cheat them _____

Name _____   GLOSSARY FILL-IN-THE-BLANK

Use a word or phrase from the box to complete each sentence. Not all words or phrases will be used.

primary	balance	fraud	credit card machine
authorized	due date	late fee	
credit limit	credit score	establish	

1. After the cashier rang up his purchases, Juan put his credit card into the _____ to check out.

2. Denise wanted to make sure to pay her credit card bill before the _____.

3. The _____ on Jason's credit card just got increased to $3,500.00.

4. Lisa hoped her _____ was over 700.

5. Zach was trying to _____ good credit so he could get another credit card.

6. Jon missed his payment date and had to pay a _____ of $35.00.

7. Maria was asked for her security code to help prevent _____.

Credit Card Math

Name _____   GLOSSARY FILL-IN-THE-BLANK

Use a word or phrase from the box to complete each sentence. Not all words or phrases will be used.

| credit history | merchant | available credit | lender | interest |
| expiration date | microchip | transactions | debt | account number |

1. There were four _____ listed on the credit card account statement.

2. If you have a bad _____ it's hard to get a credit card.

3. Kamal couldn't use his credit card after the _____.

4. Josh had too much _____ to get another credit card.

5. Since Kristin couldn't pay back all the money she borrowed within 30 days, she had to pay _____ on top of what she owed.

6. Mr. Peterson didn't have enough _____ to buy the guitar that he wanted.

7. No two people are given the same _____.

ANSWER KEY

PAGE 3
1) for extra security and to prevent fraud 2) 524 3) food, clothing, medicine, household goods 4) 000 1234 5678 9000 5) You have to pay interest. 6) Visa®, MasterCard® 7) Purchases are limited to that business. 8) by the expiration date.

PAGE 5
1) fill out an application 2) credit score, how much money you make 3) at least 18 4) in the mail 5) the primary cardholder 6) You have to give the company a cash deposit. 7) how much money you can borrow 8) credit score, how much you make, how much debt you have

PAGE 7
1) 001-23-4512 2) 3 months 3) 2001 4) 10811 E. Portabello Ave. Mesa, AZ 85260 5) Starbucks, 2 years, 1 month 6) Gold Standard Bank 7) $200.00 8) $750.00 9) Gold Standard Bank

PAGE 10
1) fill out card info at checkout 2) name, account number, expiration date, security code 3) to show how much you owe and what your minimum payment is 4) tap the credit card machine 5) by the due date on the statement 6) make small purchases 7) email or text reminders, auto bill payment 8) so you don't pay a late fee and affect your credit score

PAGE 12
1) 6036 3101 9102 8828 2) $12.18 3) 10/3 4) $2.49 5) $500.00 6) $40.00 7) 6 months 8) Nov. 10 9) up to $35.00

PAGE 15
1) a number that helps companies decide whether to loan money 2) to see how likely someone is to pay their debts 3) Experian, Transunion, Equifax 4) Banks and businesses report how you use your credit. 5) payment history 6) length of credit history 7) it can lower your credit score 8) Good

PAGE 18
1) B 2) C 3) A 4) B 5) A 6) D 7) B 8) C

PAGE 21
1) $5,400.00 2) $206.00 3) $2,919.00 4) 9/24 5) 159 2449 9654 8001 6) $6,693.00, $353.00

PAGE 22
1) $124.44, $4,175.56 2) $708.00, $3,467.56

PAGE 24
1) $726.85 2) $81.63 3) $645.22 4) $75.00 4/25 5) $281.00 6) $2.39 7) $3,414.69 8) $885.31 9) $698.31 10) $3,601.69

PAGE 25
Answers to question will vary.

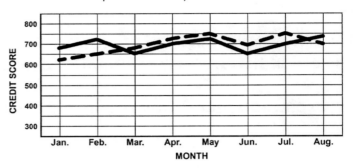

PAGE 28
1) 279 9811 0291 7753 2) $525.00 3) $3,775.00 4) $2,899.89 5) $2,406.00 6) 10/26 7) $2,209.89 8) $1,359.02

PAGE 29
1) $720.11 2) $6,050.00 3) $1,600.11 4) Valley Bank, the other two credit cards are store cards and cannot be used to buy a train ticket. 5) Valley Bank

PAGE 30
1) $141.71 2) $320.43 3) $59.50
4) **Left Column:**
65 Bennington Place
#405
Deerfield, IL
60015
Right Column:
632881710016623
01/2022   116
847-555-9219

PAGE 31
1) $58.45 2) $124.79 3) $183.24 4) $515.41 5) $1,034.59

PAGE 32

Balance Summary	
Previous Balance	$385.32
Payments	− $58.00
Other Credits	− $0.00
Cash Advances	+ $0.00
New Purchases	+$183.24
Fees Charged	+ $4.85
Interest Charged	+ $0.00
New Balance	= $514.41

Keisha Reynolds
Account Number 279 9811 0291 7753
Statement Billing Period 9/1 to 10/1

24-Hour Customer Service 1-800-555-4701
TTY for Hearing/Speech Impaired: 1-800-555-4990
Outside the US Call Collect: 1-925-555-4994
Gold Standard Bank Online: libertydepartmentstore.com

Send General Inquiries To:
PO BOX 50000, CHICAGO, IL 60007-0347

| Total Credit Limit | $1,550.00 | Total Available Credit | $1,034.59 |

Payment Information	
New Balance	$514.41
Minimum Payment	$64.00
Payment Due Date	10/28

Late Payment Warning: If we do not receive your minimum payment by the date listed above, you may have to pay a late fee up to $35.

Transactions
Trans Reference Description Charges

Purchases

Date	Type	Description	Amount
9/5	ONLINE	Sun Hat	$24.95
9/25	ONLINE	Pair of Shorts	$33.50
9/10	IN-STORE	Handbag	$43.95
9/15	IN-STORE	Scarf	$16.39
9/18	IN-STORE	Pair of Jeans	$64.45
		TOTAL NEW PURCHASES	$183.24

Credit Card Math ©Remedia Publications

ANSWER KEY

PAGE 33

1) 5 months 2) 1 month 3) 725

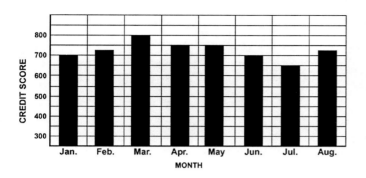

PAGE 36

1) $3,472.00 2) $868.00 3) $41,664.00 4) $2,553.61
5) 12/26 6) 10 months 7) $1,551.90 8) $13,200.00

PAGE 37

1) $8.50 2) $6,207.60 3) $581.55 4) $101.75, $83.25
5) $96.00 6) $13.95

PAGE 39

1) Mid-Century Modern 2) $78.00, $71.97 3) $42.90, $23.10 4) $4.50, $31.50 5) $47.50

PAGE 40

1) $168.40 2) $13.47 3) $197.36

PAGE 40

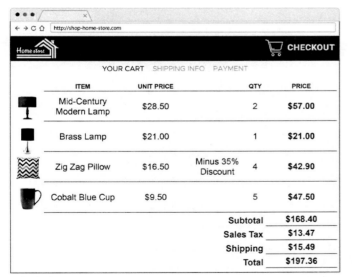

PAGE 41

Left Column:
Alex
Bailey
ACB@yahoo.com
336-555-8734
678 Birch St. #512
Greensboro, NC 27405

Right Column:
Home Store Card
Alex C. Bailey
912661225900651
02/2025
628

PAGE 44

1) 5 years, 6 months 2) $84,960.00 3) $1,770.00
4) $3,414.72 5) $3,665.28 6) $22,143.83
7) $7,114.08, $11,529.51

PAGE 45

1) $722.50 2) $34,680.00 3) $231.20, $86.70
4) $2,774.40 5) $1,040.40

PAGE 46

1) 731 1200 0381 1459, 3/22, 109
2) $119.75, $5.25, $9.58, $23.95, $153.28, $51.09

PAGE 48

1) $450.00 2) $2,399.97 3) Samsung Gear Frontier, $10.04 4) $1,869.97, $1,104.99, $524.99 5) $299.98, $99.92

PAGE 49

1) $3,274.94 2) $229.25 3) $3,520.67

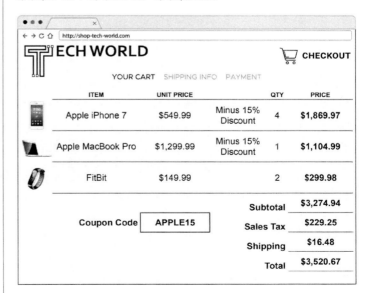

ANSWER KEY

PAGE 50

Left Column:
Carmela
Martinez
carmeladm@gmail.com
714-555-9063
1631 Orange Blossom Lane
Anaheim, CA 92801

Right Column:
MasterCard
Carmela D. Martinez
731120003811459
03/2022
109

PAGES 51-53
Answers will vary.

PAGE 56
1) balance 2) credit score 3) interest 4) expiration date
5) lender 6) debt 7) late fee 8) credit reference

PAGE 57
1) transaction 2) merchant 3) available credit
4) minimum payment 5) microchip 6) credit history
7) security code 8) fraud

PAGE 58
1) credit card machine 2) due date 3) credit limit
4) credit score 5) establish 6) late fee 7) fraud

PAGE 59
1) transactions 2) credit history 3) expiration date
4) debt 5) interest 6) available credit 7) account number